POETIC PRAISE

Poetic Praise

For Seasons of Singleness

By Patricia Middleton

POETIC PRAISE

Cover Photo by istock.com/thumb, fantom_rd
Printed in the United States of America
2016, 2023

All scripture is quoted from the New Kings James Version unless
otherwise noted.

Published By
I Write The Vision dba
Poetricia Publishing
Collingswood, N.J.

ISBN 978 0 9801286 3 5
ISBN 0 9801286 3 3

DEDICATION

To my daughter Angella:

Your life itself is a poetic praise unto God for you are
The epitome of a beautifully saved single woman:
"An example to [and of] believers in word, in conduct,
in love, in spirit, in faith, and in purity." (1 Timothy 4:12)

I still can't believe God gave me such a precious gift as you.
Love always,
Mom

Patricia ♥ Middleton

CONTENTS

POETIC PRAISE

INTRODUCTION

Poetic Praise is a collection of poems I wrote in various seasons of my singleness. Some of the poems will make you laugh. A few may make you shed a tear. Several will give you a *Selah moment* - a moment of quiet introspection. But most of them will lead you into praise.

During the intermediate years of my singleness journey I discovered the humanity of the Psalms. One study states that over 40% of the recorded Psalms are laments (expressions of sorrow and regret). My favorite example of this is Psalm 13:

A PSALM OF DAVID (A plea for deliverance)

Lord, how long will You forget me? Forever?
How long will You hide Your face from me?

How long will I store up anxious concerns within me,
agony in my mind every day?
How long will my enemy dominate me?

Consider me and answer, Lord my God.
Restore brightness to my eyes;
Otherwise, I will sleep in death.

My enemy will say, "I have triumphed over him,"
and my foes will rejoice because I am shaken.

But I have trusted in Your faithful love;
my heart will rejoice in Your deliverance.

I will sing to the Lord
because He has treated me generously.

Just like we do when it comes to our singleness, David begins this Psalm by asking God *"How long?"* four times in the first two verses. He follows with a request in verse three, and a worry in verse four. What first struck me was how honest he was with God about his fears and his impatience. But more than that, I was encouraged by how he ended the Psalm. The last two verses, like many of the lamenting Psalms, ended with praise. In spite of all the inner turmoil, fear and doubt, David sealed it all with a praise. In doing this, David paints a literal picture of *the sacrifice of praise* (Psalm 116:17).

As singles, we are called to do the same. That begins with being honest with ourselves and honest with God. Like David. Bearing everything in prayer. Confessing not only our sin, but our doubts, worries, and struggles too. God doesn't want us to deny, hide, or suppress our feelings. He wants us to give them to Him. He wants us to empty ourselves of all that baggage until nothing is left. And there, right there in that emptiness, He wants our praise.

There's a reason Isaiah 61:3 tells us that we are to *"put on the garment of praise for the spirit of heaviness."* It won't be easy, but I promise you it will be worth it. I found out that after we *"cast all our cares on Him"* (Psalms 55:22), and offer Him the sincere, heartfelt, *"sacrifice of praise"* (Hebrews 13:15), a trickle-down effect will begin that will really bless us in our singleness.

First, as we *"pour out our hearts before Him"* (Psalm 62:8) we are ushered into His presence, for *"He dwells the midst of our praise"* (Psalm 22:3). Once in His presence, we have access to *"the fullness of joy"* (Psalms 16:11). And that joy – the Lord's joy – *"is our strength"* (Nehemiah 8:10).

Did you see that? We went from pouring out our heart to God and giving Him praise, to receiving joy and strength.

That's the purpose of Poetic Praise – For Seasons of Singleness. To realize that no matter what our marital status is, we should always *"Give unto the Lord the glory that is due unto His name"* (Psalms 29:2).

Patricia ♥ Middleton

POETIC PRAISE

Patricia ♥ Middleton

I PRAY TO GOD FOR YOU

As you read each poem,
Every verse and every rhyme,
I pray to God you're blessed with,
A special peace of mind.

I pray to God no matter what,
Season of singleness you're in,
That this book of Poetic Praise,
Will lead you straight to Him.

I pray these poems uplift you,
As they have uplifted me,
I pray to God you are encouraged,
To trust God and believe.

Patricia ♥ Middleton

AND GOD

When I was a little girl,
And abuse was the center of my world,
I prayed,
And God made a way.

When I was saved at 15,
And the light of God was seen,
I prayed,
And God gave me the words to say.

When I skipped college, had twins, and then,
Entered into a life of sin,
I prayed,
And God turned my darkness into day.

When love was lost and found,
At first sight and on the rebound,
I prayed,
And God healed me from the pain.

When my life was in an economic recession,
When car and home were on the brink of
Repossession,
I prayed,

And God saved the day.
When he came into my life,
And I thought we would be husband and wife,
I prayed,
And God said "No Way!"

And because He had proven Himself all those
other times,
I obeyed.

Trust in the Lord with all your heart,
And lean not on your own understanding;
In all your ways acknowledge Him,
And He shall direct your paths.
Proverbs 3:5-6

DO YOU

Do you long for arms to hold you?
Shoulders to lay your head upon?
Ears to listen to your troubles?
Loving words encouraging you on?

Do you ever feel like you are not loved?
Do you ever think that no one cares?
Do you ever wonder why, in spite of all this,
When you call me, I AM there?

Do you ever read the words I left you?
Recorded thousands of years ago?
Have you ever felt My spirit cover you?
Have you ever felt My overflow?

If you answered yes to any of these questions,
Then you know that you are loved,
Beyond what someone else may offer,
Deeper, truer and far above.

I know that won't stop you from longing,
For romantic love – I made you this way,
But you must learn to be content,
Regardless of your current marital state.

For just as sure as I AM God someone is coming,
Who will love you the way I want you to be loved,
Who will cherish you above himself and others,
Who will be a companion sent from above.

If you can just hold on a little longer,
If you can trust that I AM in control,
If you can believe I know what I AM doing,
Someday you'll have someone to have and hold.

But those who wait on the LORD
Shall renew their strength;
They shall mount up with wings like eagles,
They shall run and not be weary,
They shall walk and not faint.
Isaiah 40:31

THE DOOR

I opened a door once in my life,
Looking for love, I stepped in.
But waiting on the other side for me,
Were pleasures wrapped in sin.

From room to room for several years,
I roamed each wicked floor,
Until I heard Jesus calling me,
From the other side of the door.

He beckoned me down each hallway,
Past every sin filled room I tried,
Ever so sweetly calling my name,
Until I was safely back outside.

Only to discover another door,
Where Jesus stood waiting for me,
Sure of His love, I stepped through that door,
And finally, I was free.

"I am the door.
If anyone enters by Me, he will be saved,
and will go in and out and find pasture."
John 10:9

FAITH SAYS (a song of faith)

When it seems like what you're waiting on,
Is never going to come
And it seems as if your dream is on eternal hold
Your mind may say walk away
But faith says hold on

When it seems like the prayer you prayed
yesterday
Is as far from coming true for you as the milky-
way
You tell yourself again and again
To let it go
But faith says hold on

Faith says hold on to the Lord, you can't go wrong
Faith says hold on to His word, until you're strong
Faith says you know you're not alone, so go on
And in Him
Be strong
Faith says hold on

Seeing isn't believing when you walk this way
Weeping may last all night long
But with each new day
Joy comes

So walk on
And in Him be strong
Faith says hold on

Faith says hold on to the Lord, you can't go wrong
Faith says hold on to His word, until you're strong
Faith says you know you're not alone, so go on
And in Him
Be strong
Faith says hold on

For we walk by faith, not by sight.
2 Corinthians 5:7

FROM JESUS, WITH LOVE

There's so much that I have to say,
There's so much that I feel,
I want to tell you that I care,
And that My love is real.

I want to let you know that I,
Would never leave your side,
I want you to know I'll always be here,
In Me you can abide.

There's more that I want you to know,
Like the fact that I understand,
And I'll always give you direction,
If you would only take My hand.

Last of all, I want to say,
If you take Me at My Word,
I'll be with you always,
Even until the end of the world.

"And remember
I am with you always,
to the end of the world."
Matthew 28:20

THE GREATEST LOVE OF ALL

For years I searched for true love,
And wondered why I could not find,
Mr. Right, Mr. Almost,
Or something close to that sound.

For years I thought a mother's love
Was THE love of them all,
So I put true love on the back burner,
And with my twins stood tall.

For years I thought – maybe family,
Was what real love was all about,
Always there, to care and to share,
Of that there was no doubt.

Then one night I found myself at the altar,
Me, a backslider on my way to hell,
That very next day, God's spirit refilled me
And now I'm here to tell:

That I've discovered a love beyond all others,
The love of Calvary,
No greater love has anyone,
Than the one who died for me.

So for years to come I know that,
Besides companion, children, and family,
The greatest love of them all,
Is the love of God that saved me.

*Greater love has no one than this,
than to lay down one's life for his friends.
John 15:13*

HIS LOVING WHISPER

Once I heard a loving whisper,
And prayed it was for me,
Up until then my ears only responded,
To whispers slightly off key.

But this whisper was different,
(The others seemed out of joint)
But I didn't have to strain to hear this whisper,
It was clear and right on point.

This whisper didn't tickle my fancy,
Or seduce me to do wrong,
Or fool me with empty promises,
It knew were untrue all along.

This whisper filled me with power,
And hope and love and peace,
This whisper even brought me,
In humble submission to my knees.

This whisper though small, is mighty,
It speaks right over my fears,
It gently blows upon me,
It dries up all my tears.

There are times when I stop listening,
And other sounds creep in,
But even then, I can still faintly hear,
This loving whisper from within.

My sheep hear my voice,
and I know them, and they follow me.
John 10:27

I GIVE YOU PRAISE (a lyrical sacrifice praise)

My heart is full of tears
But my words are full of thanks
I'm fighting back my fears
And I'm offering up my praise

Thank You Lord for it could have been
Much worse than it is now
Though I'm hurting I will make it
Even though right now I don't know how

Thank You Lord for a heart to heal
Even though it seems that I can't cope
I know as sure as there's a God
For me that means there's hope

So yes, my heart is full of fears
But my words are full of thanks
And yes, I'm fighting back these tears
But still I offer up my praise

Because praise will lead me closer to You
And away from all this pain
Praise will bring me closer to You
And to all you have ordained

And so I thank You and I praise You
For the rest of all my days
I thank You and I praise You
For the blessings and the pain

Thank You for Your forgiveness
When from Your will I strayed
And thank You for Your faithfulness
When broken to You I came

And for everything in my future
That You have already ordained
I give you praise
I give you praise
I give you praise

Why are you cast down, O my soul?
And why are you disquieted within me?
Hope in God, for I shall yet praise Him
Psalms 42:5 and 11

I HAVE SUCH A FRIEND

I was carrying a weight
That was oh so heavy to bear
I neglected to cast upon Jesus
Every burden and every care

But God gave you discernment
And with two words that you said
You broke through the wall I built
"You're Hurting" come on "Let's Pray"

God used you to bring deliverance
To heal the hurt inside of me
To strengthen my inner spirit
To bring back peace to me

I'm grateful for the freedom
And that my hurting came to an end
But I'm most grateful to God
That I have such a friend

As iron sharpens iron,
So a man sharpens the countenance of his friend.
Proverbs 27:17

I KNOW

I know now why you brought me
I know why you let me go
To share my testimony
To let other women know

That you are a God that cannot lie
What you promise, you perform
You planned great and marvelous things for us
Before the day that we were born

If only we would learn to call on you
In the spirit when we pray
And know that you will answer
And believe whatever you say

*"And they overcame .... and by the blood of the Lamb
and by the word of their testimony."*
Revelation 12:116

I KNOW MY HEART

I know the right things to say and do
I know the right way to be
But I can't stop the beating of my heart
From longing to just be me.

I know what to do and what not to do
What to say and what not to say
But I don't know how in the world
To stop my heart from feeling this way.

I know how to pray and I know how to stay
Before the Lord until victory comes
But I don't know how to stop
Wondering if he was the one.

I know that God knows my future
He knows what He'll bring to pass
But I don't know how to tell my heart
To move on and forget the past.

I've been asking the Lord to show me
If I am doing the right thing
By distancing myself from the one that I thought
Would turn out to be my king.

I've been waiting for a sign from God above
To let me know that I'm pleasing Him by
Not seeing him and not calling him
But holding it all deep inside.

All my life I've prayed for what I wanted
Always ending with "Thy will be done"
I want to be sure that I'm in His will
I want to be like Jesus, His son.

So I sit and I write and I wonder when
I'll know that what I'm doing is right
I want to be able to tell my heart
That everything will turn out alright.

"The heart is deceitful above all things,
And desperately wicked; Who can know it?
I, the LORD, search the heart, I test the mind,
Even to give every man according to his ways,
According to the fruit of his doings.
Jeremiah 17:9-10

I LAY BEFORE YOU ME

Part I

Lord I come to you with all my dreams
And everything I need
Everything I am
And all I hope to be
I come to you with all my heart
All my wants and all my cares
All that I feel and all that I love
And every one of my prayers
I lay before you everything
I lay before you me.

Lord I come to you with all my plans
Everything I want to do
All my thoughts of the present and future
I give them all to you
My calendars and timelines
Of how and when I'll get things done
My weekly and monthly and annual to do lists
I give you every one
I lay before you everything
I lay before you me.

Lord I come to you with all my regrets
Of things I haven't done
Things I thought I'd have done by now
Places I still haven't gone – souls I still haven't won
I come to you with all my sins
Everything that I've done wrong
All the weights and all the sins
I give you every one
I lay before you everything
I lay before you me.

I come to you with the shame and the guilt
That's buried deep inside
My weaknesses and failures
The things I try to hide
The things about me I don't like
The things I wish that I could change
The things rob me of my confidence
And the things that make me vain
Everything I've ever lost
And everything I've gained
I lay before you everything
I lay before you me.

Lord I come to you with everything
Everything that makes me me
Who I am presently
And who I long to be
I lay before you everything
I lay before you me.

Part II

Lord here I am before you
Giving you all of me
And in exchange I'm asking you
To give me what I need.

I need more strength, I need more joy
And Lord I need more grace
I need more peace and more power
And Lord I need more faith

I've carried myself long enough
I give you all of me
Take me, mold me, help me
Make me what I should be

I lay before you everything
I lay before you me.

*I beseech you therefore, brethren, by the mercies of God,
that you present your bodies a living sacrifice,
holy, acceptable to God, which is your reasonable service.*

Romans 12:1

I'LL KNOW, HE'LL KNOW

I won't have to cry and think,
That my hope is all in vain,
I won't have to carry around a heart,
That's broken and full of pain,
Or think that time has passed,
That I cannot regain;

I'll know.

I won't have to be afraid,
That I have shared too much,
Of how I feel and what I think,
Of love and life and such,
Of how I rarely make a move,
Without the Master's guiding touch,

I'll know.

I won't have to worry and wonder,
About how he really feels,
Or if he will be the one,
Who'll ask and bend and kneel,
And 'with this ring' prove to me,
That his love is for real,

I'll know.

He won't want me to display all my abilities,
For him to see,
The beauty that's hidden,
Deep inside of me,
The hopes and aspirations,
Of what I dream to be,

                                     He'll know.

He won't need me to persuade him,
That I am the one for him,
Who'll stand beside him,
Through thick and thin,
Who will always be content,
To simply be his rib,

                                     He'll know.

He won't need convincing,
Of what a good woman I am,
Of how on Jesus Christ,
The solid rock I stand,
Of how with me he would be,
A better man, happier man,

                                     He'll know.

Then the rib which the Lord God had taken from man
He made into a woman, and He brought her to the man.
And Adam said: "This is now bone of my bones
And flesh of my flesh;
Genesis 2:22-23

I'M GLAD THAT I FOUND YOU

My life was void and empty,
And I was all alone.
The one who I thought loved me,
Left me on my own.

I was lonely and heartbroken,
Each and every day.
I was ready to give up on love,
And then You came my way.

You promised never to leave me.
You took away worry and strife.
You gave me peace and happiness.
You even gave me a new life.

The joy You make me feel is real.
The love You have is true.
Jesus, I just want to say,
I'm glad that I found You!

We love Him because He first loved us.
1 John 4:19

IN DUE TIME

In due time I will surely reap,
The seeds of labor I now sow,
The seeds of keeping up God's standards,
The seeds of living alone.

In the meantime I'll walk uprightly,
I'll continue to live by faith,
I'll run this race with patience,
And I'll strengthen others along the way.

I will delight myself in the Lord,
Each and every day.
I will seek to know His will,
Whenever I kneel to pray.

I will overcome by the blood of Jesus,
And the words of my testimony,
I'll testify that Jesus is a keeper,
Because He has surely been keeping me.

No matter the storms that come my way,
No matter the trials and tests,
No matter how long it takes the Lord,
In due time I will be blessed.

In due time I will receive the answer to,
Unspoken, silent prayers,
In due time God will reveal to me,
The who, the what, the where.

And let us not grow weary while doing good,
for in due season we shall reap
if we do not lose heart.
Galatians 6:9

IN GOD'S OWN TIME

At times God will tell us,
There's a special blessing He will bring,
Other times we seek Him out in prayer,
Asking for a certain thing.

We know beyond a doubt,
That we will get what we prayed for,
So we rise from our knees thanking God,
Confident and sure.

But then a little time goes by,
And the blessing hasn't materialized,
We become anxious, impatient, worried,
And we fail to realize.

That sometimes God shows us the blessing,
But not how it will arrive,
Sometimes He shows us the end of the road,
But not what will occur during the ride.

So we must be patient in our waiting,
Our faith cannot grow dim,
In God's own time it will come to pass,
Whatever we've asked of Him.

God is not a man that He should lie,
So when He makes a promise to you,
Believe that He is able,
To do what He said He will do.

God is not a man, that He should lie,
Nor a son of man, that He should repent.
Has He said, and will He not do?
Or has He spoken, and will He not make it good?
Numbers 23:19

IN THE GARDEN   (a lamentation)

Part I   (It's Possible)

In the Garden,
Jesus prayed,
It was the hour right before he was betrayed
And in that Garden
Jesus said
If it be possible, let this cup be passed from me

In the Garden
He knew what was to be
In the Garden
The coming pain for you and me
And so He prayed
If it be possible, let this cup be passed from me

And so today,
Hear me, Lord I pray,
If it be possible, let this cup be passed from me
This cup of living alone
Without someone to call my own

Yes on today,
I dare to pray
If it be possible,

Let this cup be passed from me
This cup of praying for someone just for me
This cup of waiting for that person to find me

This lonely, painful cup
This empty, bitter cup

I know it's possible,
Because with you all things are possible,
And with you nothing's impossible,
So let this cup be passed from me.

Part II (Nevertheless)

In the Garden,
As Jesus prayed,
Before he got up from his knees,
He had one more thing to say,

He said
Nevertheless
You are the Father, I'm the son
And nevertheless,
And this very cup is the reason why I've come
So nevertheless,
Not my will, but Father Your will be done.

And so on today,
Before I finish this prayer
Let me dare
To do the same as Christ and say

> (Lord, You know that I'm not Jesus
> Though I'm supposed to be like Jesus
> I'm me
> And in many ways,
> This is where the similarity ends)

But on today
Father I pray
If it be possible,

Let this cup be passed from me.
Part III   (In the Garden)

Lord here I stand
Still in the garden
My own secret garden of prayer.

And in this garden
I now understand
That saying nevertheless doesn't mean
You won't do it for me.

It only means
I'm willing drink the cup
If that's what you're asking of me.

Nevertheless
Only means
I'm willing to sacrifice
Becoming someone's wife
If that's what you're asking of me

So Lord I say
Nevertheless,
To my singleness
Nevertheless
I won't love you any less

Nevertheless
I won't give you any less
Nevertheless
I won't serve you any less
If I'm single until eternity.

"Father, if it is Your will,
take this cup away from Me; nevertheless
not My will, but Yours, be done."
Luke 22:42

IT'S NOT MY TIME

I laugh, I joke, I rationalize,
But when all is said and done I cry.

As I ponder the latest news amazed,
That yet another is engaged!

And all the while I wonder why,
I'm not the one who'll become a bride?

All the while I wonder when,
My Mr. Right will step on in?

What's wrong with me, what have I done
To cause the Lord to take so long?

But then I stop and realize,
That simply put, it's not my time!

For if it were, then I would be,
Engaged to get married happily.

Simply put, it's not my time!
No matter how many tears I've cried.

No matter the years I've been alone,
It's not my time, that's up to the Lord.

But there will be a time for me,
When I'll be the one getting married.

Yes, simply put, it's not my time,
But when it is, Here comes the bride!

You will arise and have mercy on Zion;
For the time to favor her,
Yes, the set time, has come.
Psalms 102:13

JESUS GAVE ME ROSES

Jesus gave me roses,
Because right from the very start,
Like flowers brighten up a room,
He brightened up my heart.

Jesus gave me roses,
When he gave me the holy ghost,
It was a gift so undeserved,
From the one who loves me most.

I am the rose of Sharon,
And the lily of the valleys.
Song of Solomon 2:1

KEEP MY LOVE

Living deep inside of me,
Is a love so pure and true,
Waiting until the day that I,
Will finally say I do.

Sometimes this love bubbles over,
When I think I've met the one,
That I have been fashioned for,
By Jesus Christ God's Son.

Only to realize it's another case,
Of mistaken identity,
I thought he was one for me,
But instead I was deceived.

The last time as I walked away,
And checked my love supply,
I silently said this prayer,
And as I began to cry:

"Lord I need a favor,
Would You please do this for me?
Keep my love safe and sure,
Under heaven's lock and key.

"And don't allow me access,
Until the one ordained by You,
Comes into my life and declares,
'My heart's desire is You'.

"But until then, Lord, keep my love,
Believe me I have tried,
But one thing I am sure of:
You're much better at it than I".

Promise me, O women of Jerusalem,
not to awaken love until the time is right.
Song of Solomon 2:7 NLT

LET GO

The time has come,
To just let go,
Of this relationship,
Because I know;

Exactly what,
Will happen in the end,
If I continue,
To live in sin.

I try, I fail,
I love, I loose,
The time has come,
For me to choose.

I've run from God,
For so many years,
I've had too few joys,
And too many tears.

God spared my life,
So the least I can do,
Is let go of you,
And start anew.

Can two walk together, unless they are agreed?
Amos 3:3

LORD, SEND ME THE ONE

The one You know will never stray,
Who'll be with You until his dying day,
Who'll never cease to kneel and pray,
Lord, send me the one.

The one who has heavenly goals to reach,
The one who lives the sermons preached,
The one who's praying for a woman like me,
Lord, send me the one.

The one who worships in spirit and truth,
The one who knows his strength lies in You,
The one who'll love me like You do,
Lord, send me the one.

For the one who is and does all this,
He's the one I long to be with,
He's the one - I am his rib,
Lord, send me the one.

"Ask, and it will be given to you; seek, and you will find; knock, and it will be opened to you."

Matthew 7:7

LOVE, FINALLY

From my earliest recollection,
I've had the desire to be understood,
For me that meant just as much as being,
Treated kind, well, and good.

When I read passages in my old journals,
From the time when I was a teen,
My words cried out to invisible readers,
Why doesn't anyone love me?

From this boy to that one to the other,
Each one eventually spurned me,
But that never stopped me from falling,
For the next one who smiled at me.

As a woman it was more of the same,
More dangerous, more damaging, more sad,
I will never admit to another,
I've had more loves than I care to have had.

The night life gave way to the *mourning*,
When it's too bright not to see all the lies,
Staring back at me from my own mirror,
And a sadness that Maybelline could not hide.

Finally the years of searching,
Began to take their toll on my heart,
To be loved, accepted and understood,
I was no longer willing to play the part.

Right about that time I met Him,
Not realizing He was there all the time,
He saw through the nonchalant smoke screen,
He saw through the fake empty smile.

He saw underneath it all,
What none of the others could see,
That all along I just wanted,
To be loved for just being me.

And love me He did, with compassion,
Even when at first I retrieved,
He consistently patiently loved me,
Until at last in His love I believed.

Behold, I stand at the door and knock. If anyone hears My voice and opens the door, I will come in to him and dine with him, and he with Me.
Revelation 3:20

LOVE LIFTED ME

Love had done many things to me,
Some too terrible to tell,
Love almost made me take my life,
Love almost put me in hell.

Love would send me to the highest heights,
Only to bring me crashing to the ground,
Love would be there every day,
Then suddenly love was nowhere to be found.

Love told me I would be beautiful,
If only I would change,
If only I would stop or start,
If only I would rearrange.

I'd finally take two steps forward,
Then love would cause me to fall,
But I didn't know that what I thought was love,
Wasn't really love at all.

One day **LOVE** gently touched me,
With a little nudge here and there,
Before I knew what was happening,
The sadness began to clear.

LOVE lifted my eyes heavenward,
Until I was finally able to see,
Beyond the pain and heartache,
LOVE was shining back at me.

LOVE lifted the burdens from my shoulders,
LOVE softly tilted my chin,
LOVE gave me the strength I needed,
To stand back up again.

God is love.
1 John 4:8

LOVE WON'T

Love won't put more on you than you can bear,
Love sacrifices for you instead,

Love put aside its own desires,
Especially when you're already in the fire,

Love denies itself to see you sail,
Instead of causing you to fail,

And when you're on a challenging road,
Instead of adding to it, love bears the load,

Love only wants what's best for you,
And what will help you to improve,

Your life, your health and your wealth too,
That's what love does when it is true.

Love is patient and kind.
Love is not jealous or boastful or proud or rude.
It does not demand its own way.
It is not irritable, and it keeps no record of being wronged.
It does not rejoice about injustice
But rejoices whenever the truth wins out.
Love never gives up, never loses faith, is always hopeful,
And endures through every circumstance.
1 Corinthians 13:4-8 NLT

MARRIED TO JESUS

I am married to Jesus,
Because He first loved me,
I trust Him like no other,
He supplies all of my needs.

I am married to Jesus,
When I need Him - He's right there,
Morning, noon, even midnight,
I can always reach Him in prayer.

I am married to Jesus,
For the rest of all my days,
He's worthy of my devotion,
He's worthy of my praise.

I am married to Jesus,
On Him I can depend,
All my battles He promised to fight,
He'll protect me until the end.

I am married to Jesus,
I think about Him all the time,
In exchange for that He gives me,
Blessed peace of mind.

I am married to Jesus,
He will always have my love,
One day He's coming back for me,
To take me home above.

Where I will still be married to Jesus,
In that New Jerusalem,
I'll reign in that city,
Forevermore with Him.

‘

For your Maker is your husband,
The Lord of hosts is His name.
Isaiah 54:5

THE MASTER CARPENTER

Long ago I gave the Lord,
My body, mind, and soul,
I surrendered these things to Him,
Because He made me whole.

But my heart was a different story,
It was torn beyond compare,
It had been used, abused, and discarded,
Without a thought or care.

I hadn't been careful who I gave it too,
I didn't realize how fragile it was,
All I had was broken pieces,
By the time I met Jesus.

But Jesus didn't seem to mind at all,
He just took out his broom and dust pan,
And swept up the pieces of my heart,
And held them in His hands.

And there in the hands of Jesus,
Laid all the pieces of my broken heart,
While patiently I stood by waiting,
For my healing and deliverance to start.

And in the hands that blessed the fish and bread,
The hands that made blinded eyes see,
I signed over ownership of my heart to Jesus,
And He performed a miracle for me.

In the hands that loosed a mute man's tongue,
The hands that opened a deaf man's ears,
Jesus put my heart back together again,
And removed all the doubts and the fears.

In the hands that raised a girl from the dead,
The hands that healed the mother of Simon's wife,
Jesus did a spiritual bypass on me,
And gave my heart a new life.

In the hands of the Master Carpenter,
The hands that were nailed to the cross,
For all the sins that destroyed my heart,
Jesus paid the cost.

In the hands of the Master Carpenter,
With the keys to death, hell and the grave,
In the hands that hold all power,
My heart was revived and reclaimed.

In the hands that healed leprosy,
The hands that turned water to wine,
My heart and all its broken pieces,
Turned out to be just fine.

Who among all these does not know
That the hand of the Lord has done this,
In whose hand is the life of every living thing,
And the breath of all mankind?
Job 12:9-10

MR. RIGHT

While I was out in the world I was looking,
For a man named Mr. Right,
He was the one who would make me happy,
He was the one who would change my life.

So, I looked for him in night clubs,
And I searched for him while at work,
I even thought I'd find him,
When I came back to the church.

But when I rededicated myself to God,
And gave my life back to Jesus Christ,
I found out that Mr. Right,
Had been there all the time.

While I was out there looking,
He patiently stood by,
Waiting for me to notice Him,
Waiting for me to realize:

That my Mr. Right is Jesus,
He proved His love at Calvary,
Where for all the sins I'd ever done,
He died upon a tree.

And unlike a natural man, Jesus would never
Leave me for another girl,
He said He'd be with me always,
Even until the end of the world.

In this day and age, a girl needs protection,
And with Jesus, no harm comes my way,
Because His hands all power
And the keys to death, hell and the grave

Jesus alone can provide for me,
He said with Him, I'd never thirst again,
Because He would be a well of water,
Springing up within.

With Jesus I don't want for anything,
Because the truth of the matter is,
The earth is the Lord's, the fullness there of,
The world, and everything within.

Not only does Jesus supply all my needs,
But He's promised me shelter too,
He said, "One day I'll take you to a place,
Where I've prepared a mansion just for you".

Jesus is also my very best friend,
I can tell him anything,
He sticks closer than a brother,
And He never repeats a thing.

So, now when I run into old girlfriends,
And they ask me if I ever found Mr. Right,
I smile, nod my head, and say "Yes,
His name is Jesus Christ"

The Lord has appeared of old to me, saying:
"Yes, I have loved you with an everlasting love;
Therefore with loving kindness I have drawn you."
Jeremiah 31:3

MY HEART'S DESIRE

One day I read the promise in,
Psalms 37:4
"God will give you your heart's desire,
If you delight yourself in the Lord".

Quickly I wrote out a list,
Of the desires of my heart,
And went before the Lord in prayer,
Asking for the blessings He'd impart.

While waiting for those blessings,
Instead of giving me what I'd asked,
God lead me to the following verse,
To see how the blessings will come to pass.

"Commit thy ways unto the Lord",
"Trust in Him" - and Him alone,
Be delighted to do things His way,
Instead of going out on my own.

The Lord wants us to commit our ways,
Completely unto Him,
The actions that we choose to take,
And the thoughts we keep within.

We should be totally committed,
In body, mind, and soul,
Surrendering all unto Him,
And trusting in Him alone.

When we learn to say yes,
To His word, His will, and His way,
To daily be a witness,
To daily kneel and pray.

Then the blessings will come pouring in,
Then verse four will be fulfilled,
He'll give us our heart's desires,
Because we will have done His will.

Delight yourself also in the Lord,
And He shall give you the desires of your heart.
Commit your way to the Lord, Trust also in Him,
And He shall bring it to pass.
Psalms 37:4-5

THE MYSTERY OF GOD'S WILL

Jesus chose for me to live,
Without a companion so He,
Could prove to me He is all the man,
That I will ever need.

When loved ones can't be near,
Sometimes I feel alone,
Until Jesus reminds me,
He'd never leave me on my own.

From time to time my money's low,
And I start to worry and fret,
But then in the spirit sings me that old song,
"He's never failed me yet".

Even as I recall the promotion,
I still haven't gotten on my job,
Jesus steps in and shows me,
My place in Kingdom of God.

We all want the finer things in life,
Yet God allows us to go without,
To teach us to rely on Jesus,
Beyond the shadow of any doubt.

If we had everything we ever wanted,
Every desire and every whim,
When would we need a Savior?
Just where would God fit in?

Often we can't understand,
The mystery of God's will,
But He leaves some things empty,
So He'll have something to fill.

For I know the thoughts that I think toward you,
*says the L*ORD*, thoughts of peace and not of evil,*
to give you a future and a hope.
Jeremiah 29:11

REMARKABLY

I met a poet and she said to me:
"If you wait on the Lord it'll turn out remarkably."

I said in response, as a testimony:
"The brother is as fine as fine can be
And talks of nothing else but marrying me.
But the man he is does not agree
With God's plan, God's purpose, or my destiny.
That line in your poem did it for me
'If I wait on the Lord it'll turn out remarkably.'
The road ahead only God can see
So I must trust in Him and not in me.
Letting go won't be an easy thing
But I'll looked to Jesus for the strength I need.
And to like minded sisters who will share with me
Messages of hope in their poetry."

I waited patiently for the LORD;
And He inclined to me,
And heard my cry.
Psalm 40:1

THAT'S LOVE

I had been searching a long time
For the real definition of love.
My search would have already been over
If I had just stopped and looked above.

I learned the hard way that love can't be
Measured by physical compatibility.
Nor can true love be based upon
Material security.

And even though a mother's love
Is called a love beyond compare.
Because it's nurturing and understanding
The answer is not found there.

And the answer is learning to love yourself
As famous singers might have you believe.
No, learning to love yourself is not
The greatest love you can achieve.

Only when we look above will we find
The greatest love of all
For God so loved this world and He
Has proven His love by far.

His love surpasses the boundaries of
Our youthful imaginations.
And His love goes far beyond
Society's human limitations.

The almighty God that we serve
Lowered Himself to death.
Put up with all sorts of torture and then
Allowed Himself to be put to death.

No greater love hath anyone that Jesus
For He laid down His life.
And not just for a friend - He went further than that
He died for all sinful mankind.

He became a human sacrifice
He suffered, bled, died, it's true.
And not for fame and glory - He already had that
He did it for me and for you.

For all the you's who wouldn't live for Him
For all the me's who turned away.
And for all of those out there who don't know yet
We've got to show them the way.

Because many people think they can find love
Anywhere from online dating sites to night clubs,
We must point them to that old rugged cross
So they'll stop and they'll say, "That's love."

And our relatives, neighbors, and coworkers
Anyone and everyone we can think of,
Should know that Jesus died for their sins
So they'll stop and they'll say, "That's love."

This world, with its mixed up messages
Looking in all the wrong places for love,
Their search would already be over
If they would just stop and look above.

That's love.

For God so loved the world that He gave
His only begotten Son, that whoever believes in Him should
not perish but have everlasting life.
John 3:16

THIS LOVE

I've found a love I cherish,
Far more than words can say,
A sweet, kind, precious love,
That takes my breath away.

This love is a love I can depend on,
No matter what I'm going through,
This love guides and directs me,
So I'll know just what to do.

This love is truly faithful,
Even when I 'm in the wrong,
It calls me, corrects me, and forgives me,
And loves me all along.

This love is ageless,
It's been here since the beginning of time,
From everlasting to everlasting,
It will live on even after I die.

This love is a true love,
It's the love that saved my life,
This love is unconditional,
It's the love of Jesus Christ.

If you long for this kind of love,
Just seek God out in prayer,
And you will find the love I found,
Waiting to meet you there.

His banner (covering) over me is love.
Song of Solomon 2:4

THY WILL BE DONE

I am not looking,
For a husband right now,
I'm getting into the Lord,
And He's showing me how,

To rely on Him,
Totally,
He will supply,
All my needs.

He's led me this far,
It's all in His hands,
He will send me,
A godly man.

Notice I said *send*,
And not *lead me to*,
I'm not going to search,
Because I'm not supposed to.

Why not browse?
Start looking anyway?
Do some window shopping?
That's what some folks say.

Well, what good is it to look
If I'm not going to buy?
I said it's all in God's hand,
And I'll tell you why:

God said "A man that finds a wife,
Finds a good thing,"
If I wait on the Lord,
A blessing He'll bring.

It's God's will be done,
Not mine and not yours,
We can ask what we want,
But the choice is the Lords.

He who is unmarried cares for the things of the Lord—
How he may please the Lord.
She who is unmarried cares about the things of the Lord,
That she may be holy both in body and in spirit.
1 Corinthians 7:32,34

TRUE LOVE

I remember the time in my life,
When I thought I was in love,
But as I look back now I can see,
I didn't know what love was.

Back then I thought love was romance,
I thought it was so sweet,
To be wined and dined every weekend,
To be swept off of my feet.

I was under the silly impression,
That love was this feeling inside,
Butterflies, goose-bumps, chills and thrills,
And girl, that look in his eyes!

I wrote then about how life wasn't worth living,
If you didn't have a love all of your own,
Until the one who I thought loved me,
Up and left me all alone.

Like a plane out of fuel I took a nose dive,
No more floating in the clouds,
I was miserable, pathetic, and lonely,
And all I did was mope around.

Then one day I met a guy named Jesus,
For Him it was love at first sight,
But for me, I played hard to get,
I was still hurting deep down inside.

Well, this Jesus, he's a guy like no other,
He began calling me every day,
At home, at work, it didn't matter,
Even though He knew I had nothing to say.

I tried to keep Him at arm's length,
I'd been hurt so many times before,
All those times I thought I'd found true love,
It was more than I'd bargained for.

Then one day I called Him,
And it was like, He'd been waiting for my call,
I began reading everything He'd written me,
And I knew I was starting to fall.

Jesus, He was always the gentleman,
He never, ever forced Himself on me,
He said "If you are heavy laden,
You can find rest if you come unto me".

He said "Don't you know how much I love you?
I gave My life just for you
And now I want to give you a new life
And mend your broken heart too"

Now I know what true love is,
It's giving and waiting patiently,
It's just being there for someone,
Like Jesus has been there for me.

It's friendship and it's laughter,
It's always doing the right thing,
It's being concerned about the future,
And what eternity will bring.

True love is more than just romance,
It's a commitment meant for life,
It's more than just being wined and dined,
And pressuring someone to be their wife.

True love is binding spiritually,
And always seeking to please each other,
It's dependable and trustworthy,
And it sticks closer than any brother.

When I fell in love with Jesus,
I fell in love with Him for keeps,
I knew all along that His love was true,
Once I knew about Calvary.

*But God demonstrates His own love toward us,
in that while we were still sinners, Christ died for us.*
Romans 5:8

VICTORY

Yes, I may be hurting
but the victory is mine
because I've learned to be obedient
and I've learned to sacrifice

Sure, I'm disappointed
but I still have the victory
because I've traded in what I want
for what God wants for me

And yes, I may be crying
but my victory is won
cause mingled with tears of what could have been
are tears of joy for what's to come

But thanks be to God, who gives us the victory through our Lord Jesus Christ.
1 Corinthians 15:57

WHAT IF?

"*I only need one'*
Was my confident reply
To the man-shortage comment
She used to explain
The fact that my
Marital status still
Hadn't changed.

But as I turned to walk away
I began thinking
If that's the case
Then she's right
I am doomed.

What if my 'only one'
Saved and sanctified brother
Up and married another'?
What if God has yet to point me out to him?
What if he's still living in a world of sin?

What if he was presented to me
And I murmured "*He's not my cup of tea*"?
What if he just couldn't tell me the truth:
"*I'm just not that into you*"?

Whatever the reason
Whatever the cause
My chin dipped
My eyes dripped
As I continued to ponder my list of "What ifs"

And my confident shoulders
Slumped just a little
As I began to walk away....

For my thoughts are not your thoughts, neither are your ways my ways, saith the Lord. For as the heavens are higher than the earth, so are my ways higher than your ways, and my thoughts than your thoughts.
Isaiah 55:8-9

WHEN MY HEART WRITES A LOVE POEM

When my heart writes a love poem,
I don't have to search for words,
I just stop and sit still until,
My heartbeats can be heard.

As I listen to my heartbeats,
And feel the rhythm of each one,
My heart becomes my hand,
And my pen becomes my tongue.

Slowly my lips begin to curl,
And then they break out into a smile,
As I recall the heights and depths,
Of a love quite worth the while.

Next comes a sigh from deep within,
The recesses of my soul,
As I feel again love's healing balm,
Of crevices now made whole.

Finally I clear my throat,
In an effort to begin,
And I open my mouth to speak aloud,
Of how love rescued me from sin.

See, sin had my heart in bondage,
For many, many years,
Sin caused my heart first to rejoice,
Then to break out in tears.

But love broke through the haze,
Of all the hurt and shame and blame,
And all it demanded in return,
Is that I declare its name: "JESUS! "

My mouth now closed is still smiling,
My chest heaves out one more sigh,
Once again I'm listening to my heartbeats,
But now you know the reason why.

I will praise you, O Lord, with all my heart;
I will tell of all your wonders.
Psalms 9:1

I love you O Lord, You are my strength.
Psalms 18:1

WHEN YOU SIN (a song of repentance)

(Verse)
I sinned again
I broke the heart of my Lord, my love, my friend
I sinned again
When I would do what is good,
Instead I sin
But tell me who do you cry do when you sin?

(Verse)
I sinned again
It's harder to resist than to give in
So I give in - and sin again
I crucified my Savior once again
Now where do I go if not to him?
But who do you cry to when you sin?
When you do something you said you'd never do again?
What then?
Tell me who do you cry to when you sin?

(Bridge)
If any man sin
We have an advocate in Jesus for our sin
Confess what you've done
He will forgive us
You can still cry unto Him when you have sinned

(Bridge)
If any man sin
Confide and hide in Him until you're whole again
Confess what you've done
He will forgive us
You can still cry unto Him when you have sinned

(Chorus)
Cry Lord have mercy on me
Extend your grace unto me
Don't just forgive me
But will you cleanse me
Cause I don't want to crucify you Lord again

Father I pray
Lord have mercy on me
Extend your grace unto me
Don't just forgive me
But will you cleanse me
Because I want to feel Your spirit once again

Don't just forgive me
But will you cleanse me
I can still cry unto You when I sin

If we confess our sins, He is faithful and just
to forgive us our sins and to cleanse us
from all unrighteousness.
1 John 1:9

WITH A MADE UP MIND

With a made up mind,
And strength anew,
With peace inside,
I'm leaving you.

With a made up mind,
And a made up heart,
I realize I can,
Make a new start.

With a made up mind,
Now I know,
Without a doubt,
I can let go.

With a made up mind,
And a made up plan,
With the help of the Lord,
I know I can.

The love I need,
You cannot give,
So with a made up mind,
For God I'll live.

Don't team up with those who are unbelievers.
How can righteousness be a partner with wickedness? How
can light live with darkness??
2 Corinthians 6:14

YOU ALONE

As a deer pants for water
So pants my soul after Thee.
My soul thrists for You alone
Because You set me free.

You alone, Lord Jesus Christ
Loved me way back when,
I didn't even love myself
So filthy I was from sin.

But You alone didn't hesitate
To cleanse me with your blood.
And set me in heavenly places
I never before dreamed of.

You alone empower me
With Your Spirit every day.
You alone know I can't see
And so You lead the way.

You alone fill the darkness
With the protection of Your word.
I can sleep through nights in peace
Little voices now unheard.

You alone, My Messiah
Know the joys and pains inside.
And You alone beckon me
Beneath Your wings to hide.

You alone, are my true love
How could I want for more?
When in the spirit You sing to me
Songs I've never heard before?

You alone, Lord of my life
I live to do Your will.
Knowing that if I seek you first
Unspoken prayers will be fulfilled.

You alone, oh Most High God
I'm Your living sacrifice,
Holy and acceptable to You alone
My heart, my soul, my mind.

You alone, Lord, are my King
And I give you all the praise,
For You alone are worthy
Far more than words can say.

You alone, Lord, You alone,
I pledge my love to You,
Not just with these rhyming words
But Your commandments I will do.

As a deer pants for water
So pants my soul after Thee.
My soul thrists for You alone
Because You set me free.

As the deer pants for the water brooks,
So pants my soul for You, O God.
My soul thirsts for God, for the living God.
Psalms 42:1-2

YOU ARE THERE (a song of praise)

Sometimes it seems
The weight is more than I can bear
And I open my mouth to say
Life isn't fair
But You are there
Lord, You are there.

The days I smile as if I haven't
Got a care
The nights my soul cries out
In deep despair
You are there
Lord you are there.

There
Whenever I just need a friend,
You've shown me
Time and time again
That You'll be there.

There
When satan tries to tell me to beware
You're there,
You give me the strength I need
To take the dare.

There
Taking the time to show me that You care
Waiting for me when I kneel in prayer
Lord You are there
You're always there.

I reach my hand to You to lead the way
I love You more than words could ever say
Because You are there
You're always there.

And no one in this world could ever compare
To You
Because You are there
Lord You are there
You're always there.

Fear not, for I am with you;
Be not dismayed, for I am your God.
I will strengthen you, Yes, I will help you,
I will uphold you with My righteous right hand.
Isaiah 41:10

YOU STILL SAVED ME

I'm thankful to You,
Keeper when I don't want to be kept,
You still covered me,
Made a way of escape,
When I thought I passed the point of no return,
When I rejected Your love in search of another,
You didn't reject me,
You still loved me,
Knowing that I would turn away, risk it all,
You still saved me.

Thank You.

*God's mercy is so abundant, and His love for us is
so great, that while we were spiritually dead in our
disobedience, He brought us to life with Christ.
It is by God's grace that you have been saved.*
Ephesians 2:4

Thank you for reading Poetic Praise,

And remember:

Above all else, guard your heart,
for everything you do flows from it.
Proverbs 4:23 NIV

Patricia ❤ Middleton

ABOUT THE AUTHOR

Patricia Middleton is a uniquely gifted inspirational speaker, workshop leader and Christian educator. After 20 years in the telecommunications industry, Patricia began a new career as a radio host with WTMR 800 AM (Beasley Media Group). A few years later she became a publishing consultant by starting her own company, Poetricia Publishing. Since then she has written 10 books and assisted almost 30 other writers in becoming self-published authors.

Patricia is certified with the New Jersey Coalition to End Domestic Violence and uses her platforms to give voice to the horrors of domestic violence and the hope found in its aftermath. She also partners with senior living facilities, local libraries, and community and faith-based organizations to facilitate virtual and in-person poetry and writing workshops. During the pandemic, she launched The Village Authors, a virtual gathering of aspiring, new and seasoned authors in pursuit of writing well, and WPAT Live! a faith-based podcast.

Her motto is, "I've written my vision; let me help you write yours."

Find out more at www.patriciamiddleton.com.

Patricia ♥ Middleton

ALSO BY PATRICIA MIDDLETON

A TIME TO WRITE (2010)
Inspirational Poems and Songs of Worship.

THE WRITING WAS ON THE WALL (2013)
But I Didn't Know the Signs (of Dating Violence)

WORDS WILL NEVER HURT ME (2013)
Childhood Memories of Domestic Violence

LOVE LINES (2016)
Inspirational Wedding Poems

WORDBEATS (2016)
The Pulsations of a Poet's Heart

MR. WRITE (2019)
Poems of Love and Loss

FIFTY MINUTES OF GRACE (2020)
And Other Stories of God's Undeserved Favor

IT IS WRITTEN (2020)
New and Selected Poems

BEHIND THE RHYME (2023)
Poems & Prompts

Patricia ♥ Middleton